Introduction

The *Cambridge Primary Science* series has been developed to match the Cambridge International Examinations Primary Science curriculum framework. It is a fun, flexible and easy to use course that gives both learners and teachers the support they need. In keeping with the aims of the curriculum itself, it encourages learners to be actively engaged with the content, and develop enquiry skills as well as subject knowledge.

This Activity Book for Stage 5 is designed to be used alongside the Learner's Book for the same stage, ISBN 978-1-107-66304-6.

In this book you will find an exercise to accompany each topic presented in the Learner's Book, as well as a language review exercise at the end of each unit to practise the key vocabulary. The exercises are designed to be completed as pen-and-paper exercises, and learners can work on them individually or in pairs or small groups. You can set the exercises as in-class work or homework.

There are different styles of exercise throughout to maintain interest and to suit different purposes. The main aims of the exercises in this book are:

- to consolidate the subject knowledge presented in the Learner's Book
- to encourage learners to apply the knowledge in new situations, thus developing understanding
- to practise scientific language
- to develop scientific enquiry skills such as presenting and interpreting results from investigations.

The answers to the exercises in this Activity Book are available in the Teacher's Resource for Stage 5, ISBN 978-1-107-67673-2. This resource also contains extensive guidance on all the topics, ideas for classroom activities, and guidance notes on all the activities presented in the Learners' Book. You will also find a large collection of worksheets.

We hope you enjoy using this series.

With best wishes,
the Cambridge Primary Science team.

Contents

CAMBRIDGE PRIMARY
Science

Activity Book

5

Fiona Baxter and Liz Dilley

CAMBRIDGE
UNIVERSITY PRESS

University Printing House, Cambridge CB2 8BS, United Kingdom

Cambridge University Press is part of the University of Cambridge.

It furthers the University's mission by disseminating knowledge in the pursuit of education, learning and research at the highest international levels of excellence.

www.cambridge.org
Information on this title: www.cambridge.org/9781107658974

© Cambridge University Press 2014

First published 2014
3rd printing 2014

Printed in the United Kingdom by Short Run Press, Exeter

A catalogue record for this publication is available from the British Library

ISBN 978-1-107-65897-4 Paperback

Additional resources for this publication at www.cambridge.org/delange

The publisher is grateful to the experienced teachers Mansoora Shoaib Shah, Lahore Grammar School, 55 Main, Gulberg, Lahore and Lynne Ransford for their careful reviewing of the content.

Cover artwork: Bill Bolton

Useful words

analyse	to comment on and explain data
	Latif could tell everyone where it would rain tomorrow because he was able to **analyse** the weather map.
apply	to use your knowledge that you already have to explain something new
	Aruna was able to **apply** what she knew about evaporation to solve the problem.
conclusion	something you decide after looking at all the information you have
	Ashok's **conclusion** was that water evaporates faster when the wind blows.
data	information presented in the form of a table, a graph or lists
	This table of **data** shows the times of sunrise and sunset for the month of June.
decide	to choose one thing instead of another
	Zainab and Fatima could not **decide** which fabric to buy.
decrease	to get smaller in amount or number
	The number of children at school will **decrease** when people get the flu and stay at home.

demonstrate	to show

The teacher used a pan of water to **demonstrate** how water boils.

describe	to say what something is like

Ming used the words fluffy, white and friendly to **describe** her kitten.

estimate	to make a rough calculation

Ali was not wearing his watch. He made an **estimate** of the time.

evidence	signs or information which show that something is true

Mina collected **evidence** from her investigation to show that seeds need water to germinate.

identify	to recognise and correctly name something or someone

Rafaela could **identify** the flower by the colour and shape of its petals.

improve	to make better

Gizela was able to **improve** her times for swimming 400 metres.

increase	to get bigger in amount or number

The temperature began to **increase** as the water was heated.

interpret	to explain the meaning of something

Bo was able to **interpret** the results of the investigation to mean that plants need light to grow.

Useful words

invent	to design something or think of something for the first time
	Many people have been able to **invent** useful products.
label	to name parts of a diagram
	Label the different parts of the plant in this diagram.
moist	slightly wet
	Seeds grow better in soil that is **moist** but not wet.
pattern	something that repeats itself in a way you can predict
	The **pattern** that Leo observed in his results was that seeds with long straight wings stay in the air longer.
product	something that is made for a certain use
	A **product** that we use at school is paper.
similarity	when things are the same in some way
	A **similarity** between Josh and Leah is that they are both left-handed.
unit	a standard measurement
	The **unit** of measurement for electric current is the ampere.

Investigating plant growth

Exercise 1.1 Seeds

In this exercise, you will revise what you know about seeds.

1 Who is right about the pumpkin? Say why.

_____

_____

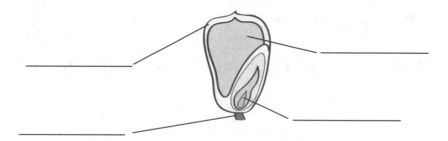

A pumpkin is a fruit, Luisa.

It's not a fruit, Maria. Pumpkin is not sweet.

2 Label the drawing of a maize seed.

3 Write the job of each part of the seed below its label. Use this list to help you.

- Grows into a new plant.
- Protects the seed.

- Joins the seed to the fruit.
- Gives the seed energy to grow.

Exercise 1.2 How seeds grow

In this exercise, you will think about the stages of seed germination.

1 The pictures of the stages of seed germination are in the wrong order.

Decide what order the pictures should go in, and number them 1–5.

Use the descriptions below to label each stage.

The first root grows

Leaves get bigger and seeds shrivel

The first leaves grow

Seed coat splits

The first shoot grows

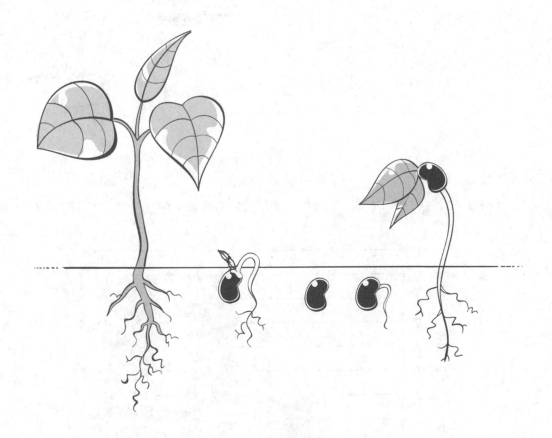

2 Is any stage of germination missing? If so, which stage?

Exercise 1.3 Investigating germination

In this exercise, you will look at a bar chart to answer questions about seed germination.

Class 5 investigated germination. They put seeds on damp cotton wool into plastic bags. They put the plastic bags in different places.

They checked the seeds after three days. This is a bar chart of their results.

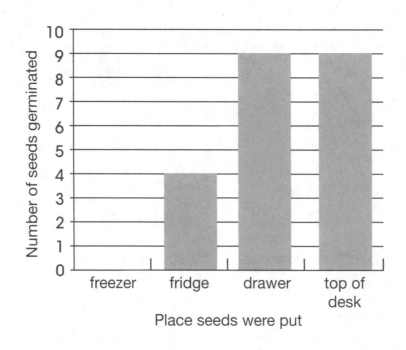

1 Where did the most seeds germinate? _____

2 Where did the fewest seeds germinate? _____

3 Suggest a reason why the same number of seeds germinated in the drawer as on the top of the desk.

_____

_____

_____

_____

4 What do the results tell you about the conditions that seeds need to germinate?

_____

_____

_____

_____

5 Predict what would happen to the number of seeds that germinate in the drawer if you suck all the air from the plastic bag that they are in.

_____

_____

_____

_____

In this exercise, you will think about what plants need to grow.

1 Lulu's tomato plants are not growing well and the leaves are yellow. Suggest **two** things that she can do to help her tomato plants to grow better.

_____

_____

2 Lulu noticed that many plants in her garden grow better in summer than in winter. Suggest a reason for this.

_____

_____

3 Fill in the labels on the drawing to show the factors that Lulu's plants need for growth.

Exercise 1.5 Investigating plant growth

In this exercise, you will think about an investigation of plant growth.

Akia and Dembe did an investigation to find out if plants can grow in the dark. They watered the plants and measured their growth. This is a chart of their results.

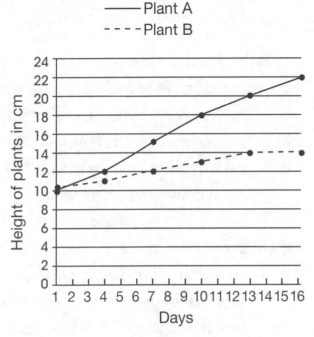

1 Briefly describe how they could have carried out their investigation to make it a fair test.

_____

_____

_____

2 How tall were the plants at the start? _____

3 How often did they measure the plants? _____

4 a Which plant grew the most? _____

  b How tall did it grow? _____

  c Was this plant in the dark or the light? Explain how you know this.

_____

_____

5 Write a conclusion for the investigation.

_____

_____

Language review

This exercise checks that you understand the scientific words used in this unit.

Find the words in the word search that have these meanings.

a   part of a plant that can grow into new plant

b   the tiny plant inside a seed that grows into a new plant

c   the outer cover that protects the seed

d   the way things are in the environment

e   when a seed starts to grow

f   to take in a substance

g   to become small and very dry

h   something that cause changes

i   needed for growth by plants but not seeds

j   provides energy for germination

One of the words has been written backwards.

G	E	R	M	I	N	A	T	E	P	L
Q	M	W	E	R	T	B	Y	U	I	O
A	B	S	D	F	G	S	E	E	D	H
J	R	K	L	G	I	O	A	X	C	B
B	Y	N	N	S	H	R	I	V	E	L
T	O	M	D	A	J	B	O	P	H	I
E	R	O	T	S	D	O	O	F	K	G
S	D	S	E	E	D	C	O	A	T	H
F	A	W	E	R	T	Y	O	C	G	T
C	B	N	F	R	H	U	D	T	S	A
V	C	O	N	D	I	T	I	O	N	S
U	T	W	Z	N	L	H	Y	R	O	I

The life cycle of flowering plants

Exercise 2.1 **Why plants have flowers**

In this exercise, you will think about how flowers help plants to reproduce.

1 The diagram shows how flowers help plants to reproduce and form new plants.

Use the words in the box to help you label the diagram.

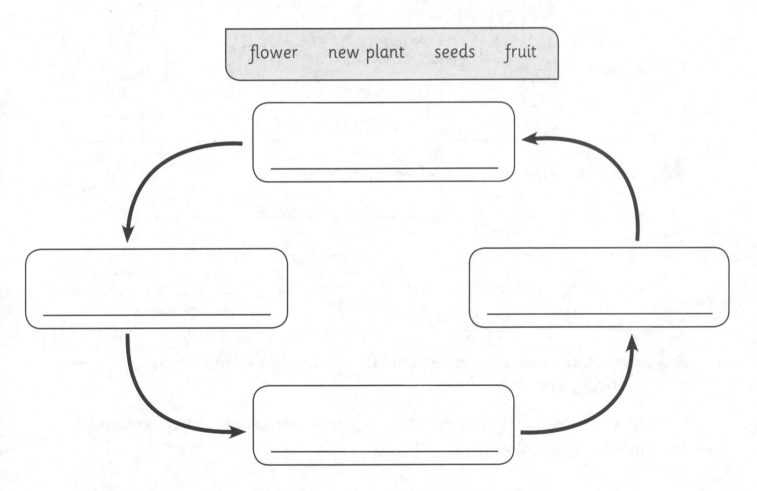

flower   new plant   seeds   fruit

2 How do flowers help plants to reproduce?

_____

_____

Exercise 2.2 How seeds are spread

In this exercise, you will match different seeds to the animals that disperse them and explain how the seeds are dispersed.

1 Draw lines to match the seeds with the animal that disperses the seeds

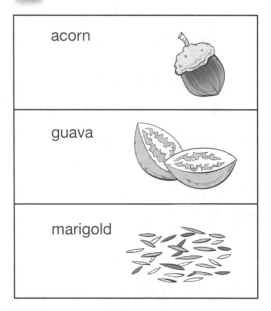

2 Explain how the parrot disperses seeds.

_____

_____

_____

_____

3 Unwanted plants that come from other places are referred to as 'alien plants'.

How can people spread the seeds of these alien plants without knowing that they are doing this?

_____

_____

_____

_____

Exercise 2.3 Other ways seeds are spread

In this exercise, you will think about how seeds are dispersed and sort them into groups.

1 How are these seeds dispersed? Sort them into groups and write the names of the seeds in the table.

Coconut   Impatiens   Lantana   Mangrove   Blackjack

Dandelion   Plum   Jacaranda   Acacia   Sycamore

Eaten	Stick on	Fly away	Float	Explode

2 How is the blackjack seed suited to its method of dispersal?

_____

_____

3 How is the sycamore seed suited to its method of dispersal?

_____

Exercise 2.4 The parts of a flower

In this exercise, you will label a drawing of a flower.

1 Label the different parts of the flower. Use these words to help you.

| petals | sepal | stigma | ovary | anther | stamen | carpel |

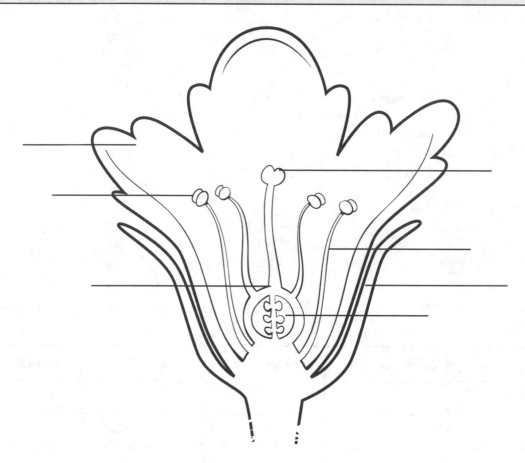

2 **a** Name the male parts of the flower.

_____

_____

b Name the female parts of the flower.

_____

_____

Exercise 2.5 Pollination

In this exercise, you will complete sentences about pollination and fertilisation.

Use the words in the box to help you complete the sentences.

You will use some words more than once.

wind   insects   seeds   pollen   stigma   anthers
nectar   anthers   ovary   fertilisation

1 The _____ of flowers make a yellow powder called _____ .

2 Pollination happens when pollen moves from the _____ to the _____ of a flower of the same type.

3 Some plants use _____ to blow the pollen far way.

4 Insects get _____ on their bodies when they visit flowers to feed on _____ .

5 The _____ and eggs join together inside the _____ during _____ .This is how _____ form.

6 The _____ becomes the fruit.

Exercise 2.6 Investigating pollination

In this exercise, you will find information about pollination from a chart.

Class 5 investigated pollination by insects. They observed the number of times different insects visited flowers in the school grounds. They drew this chart of their results.

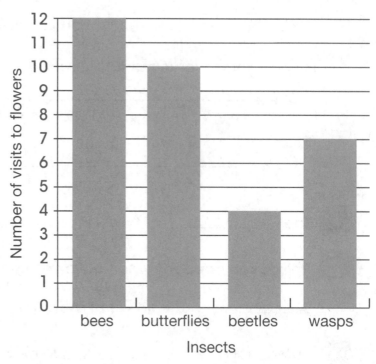

1 Which insects visited the flowers the most times?

_____

2 Which insects visited the flowers the fewest times?

_____

3 How many times did butterflies visit the flowers?

_____

4 Name three things that attract insects to flowers.

_____

5 Explain why pollination is important to plants.

_____

_____

_____

Exercise 2.7 Plant life cycles

In this exercise, you will put the processes in a plant's life cycle in the correct order.

1 Put the processes in the pumpkin plant's life cycle in the correct order.

They are shown in the box below. Number them 1–7.

2 Use the words in the box to label each process in the plant's life cycle.

| fruit and seed formation | fertilisation | growth | pollination |
| germination | flowering | seed dispersal | |

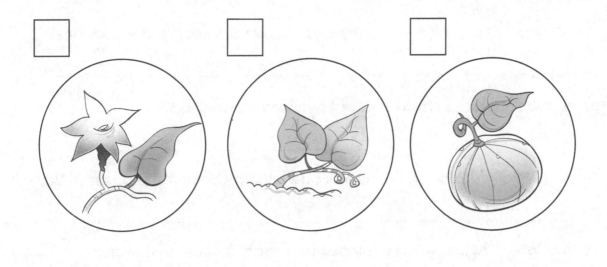

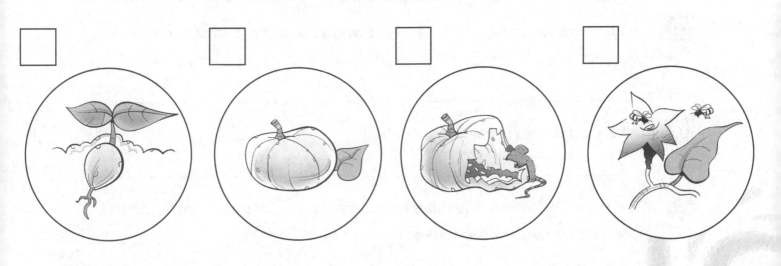

Language review

This exercise checks that you understand the scientific words used in this unit.

Look at the balloons. Each balloon contains a key word from this unit. Use the words to answer the questions. You will have to use some words more than once.

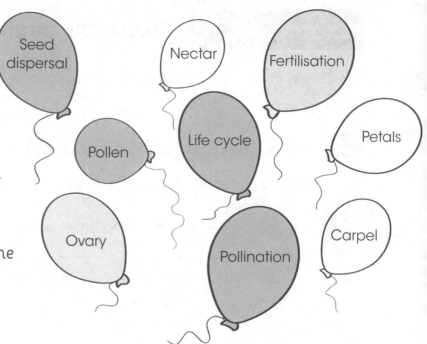

1 What process is carried out by animals, wind, water and explosions?

_____

2 **a** What process is carried out by insects and wind?

_____

b Which substance do insects and wind move in the process in 2a?

_____

c Which two words are things that attract insects to flowers?

_____

3 Which word describes what happens when the male and female parts join?

_____

4 Which part of the flower forms the fruit?

_____

5 Which word describes the different stages in a plant's life from when it grows from a seed until it makes its own seeds?

_____

3 States of matter

Exercise 3.1   Evaporation

In this exercise, you will think about what evaporation is and how it happens.

1   **Complete these sentences. Choose the correct word when there is a choice.**

Evaporation occurs when a _____ turns into a

_____. The particles in the _____

gain/lose _____ and move faster/slower and closer

together/further apart until some of them escape from the surface and

become a _____ .

2   **Cement in a cement mixer is a liquid. The cement between bricks in a wall is a solid. What has happened to the liquid in the cement?**

_____

_____

_____

3   **Why do puddles dry up quicker on hot days?**

_____

_____

_____

Exercise 3.2 Why evaporation is useful

In this exercise, you will use your knowledge of evaporation to help you to design a food product.

Akia's grandmother has ten peach trees. She cannot eat all the peaches but she does not want to waste the fruit. Akia and Dembe want to make a food product from the peaches but are not sure what to do. Can you help them?

1 Suggest a food product that Akia and Dembe can make from the peaches by using evaporation.

_____

2 Give them some ideas about how they can make their food product.
   a   What equipment could they use?

_____

_____

_____

_____

   b   How can they make sure enough evaporation takes place?
        Suggest **two** different ways.

_____

_____

_____

_____

3 Think of an example when evaporation is not useful to us.

_____

_____

_____

Exercise 3.3 Investigating evaporation

In this exercise, you will identify factors that affect evaporation, do calculations and think about what makes a fair test.

Class 5 investigated how much water evaporated from different containers after two days.

 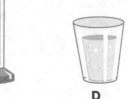

Here are their results.

Container	Volume of water at start in ml	Volume of water after two days in ml	Volume of water evaporated in ml
A	100	60	
B	40	0	
C	100	80	
D	100	50	

1   a   Complete the last column of the table.

     b   What kind of chart would you draw to show these results?

_____

2   a   In which container did the least amount of water evaporate?

_____

     b   Suggest a reason why this happened.

_____

3   Was this a fair test? Say why or why not.

_____

_____

Exercise 3.4 Investigating evaporation from a solution

In this exercise, you will revise what you know about evaporation from solutions.

Ahmed is writing a report on an investigation. Help him complete his report. Use the words in the box to help you.

> salt   water   solution   evaporated   evaporating
> evaporation   warm   dissolved

Aim

We wanted to find out if you can get salt back from a

_____ by _____ .

Method

We _____ some salt in _____

to make a salt _____ and left in a

_____ place for a few days.

Results

After a few days there was _____ in the bottom

of the container. There was no _____. It had

_____.

Conclusion

We found that we can get _____ back from a

_____ by _____ the water.

Exercise 3.5 Condensation

In this exercise, you will revise what you know about condensation.

Luisa made a solution of sugar and water in a jar. She put the lid on the jar and left it in a warm place overnight. The next day she opened the jar and saw that the inside of the lid was wet.

1 What liquid was on the inside of the lid? _____

2 Where did the liquid come from? _____

3 Name the process that made the liquid form on the inside of the lid.

_____

4 Explain how this process made the liquid form.

_____

_____

_____

5 a Which process is the reverse of the process you named in **3** ?

_____

b Would the drops of liquid have formed without the reverse process? Say why or why not.

_____

_____

_____

6 Will the liquid on the inside of the lid taste sweet? Say why or why not.

_____

_____

_____

Exercise 3.6 The water cycle

In this exercise, you will think about the water cycle.

1 Complete the sentences in the boxes about the water cycle. Use the words in the list to help you and the diagram in the Learner's Book.

> cools water vapour liquid water clouds
> evaporates condenses heated rain rises

Water on the Earth's surface is _____ and

_____ into the air as _____ .

The air _____ as it rises. Some of the

water vapour in the air _____ . Drops of

_____ in the air form _____ .

Drops of _____ fall from clouds as

_____ . _____ water returns to

the Earth this way.

2 Name **two** other ways that water can return to the Earth.

_____

Exercise 3.7 Boiling

In this exercise, you will think about what happens when a liquid boils.

Look at the pictures of beakers in a classroom.

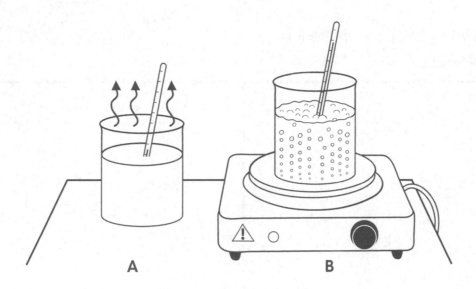

A   B

1 Which drawing shows boiling? _____

2 What process does the other drawing show? _____

3 a Write down one thing that is the same about the two processes.

_____

b Write down one thing that is different about the two processes.

_____

4 Predict what you think the temperature will be in:

a Beaker A _____

b Beaker B _____

Exercise 3.8 Melting

In this exercise, you will think about what happens when something melts.

Meng put a block of ice on a saucer.

1 Draw what happens to the ice in the boxes below.

after two minutes	after ten minutes

2 a   What has happened to the ice?

_____

b   Why did this process happen?

_____

c   At what temperature does this process happen? _____

d   What do we call this temperature? _____

3 Predict the temperature in the saucer after ten minutes.

_____

Who invented the temperature scale?

In this exercise, you will revise what you know about the history of temperature scales.

1 Draw lines to match the scientist with the temperature scale they invented.

Fahrenheit		measures boiling point of water as 373°
Celsius		measures boiling point of water as 212°
Kelvin		measures boiling point of water as 100°

2 What is the melting point of ice on each temperature scale?

a Fahrenheit _____

b Celsius _____

c Kelvin _____

3 a Mark the following temperatures on the thermometer.

Human body temperature: 37°
Melting point of candle wax: 60°
Boiling point of water: 100°

b Which temperature scale does the thermometer use?

_____

Language review

This exercise checks that you understand the scientific words used in this unit.

1 Fill in the missing words on the diagram. Use these words.

freezing   melting   evaporation   condensing

_____   _____

ice   water   water vapour

_____   _____

2 Complete these sentences. Use these words.

heat   boiling point   cool   freezing point   steam   water

If you _____ water to a temperature of 100°C it

reaches its _____ .

If you _____ ice to a temperature of 0°C it reaches

its _____ .

Liquid water forms _____ when it boils.

Ice forms _____ when it melts.

Exercise 4.1 Light travels from a source

In this exercise, you will practise what you have learnt about light travelling from a source and how we see things.

1 Seymour is looking at some trees.

    a Identify the source of light.

_____

    b Draw lines with arrows to show how Seymour sees the tree.

2 Safiya is looking at a book.

    a Identify the source of light.

_____

    b Draw lines with arrows to show how Safiya sees the book.

Exercise 4.2 Mirrors

In this exercise, you will revise what you have learnt so far about light reflecting off mirrors.

The diagrams show light reflecting off mirrors. Complete each of the diagrams by adding the light arriving at the mirror or the light reflecting off the mirror.

Make sure that you draw the arrows correctly.

Add these labels to each diagram.

light from source   reflected light

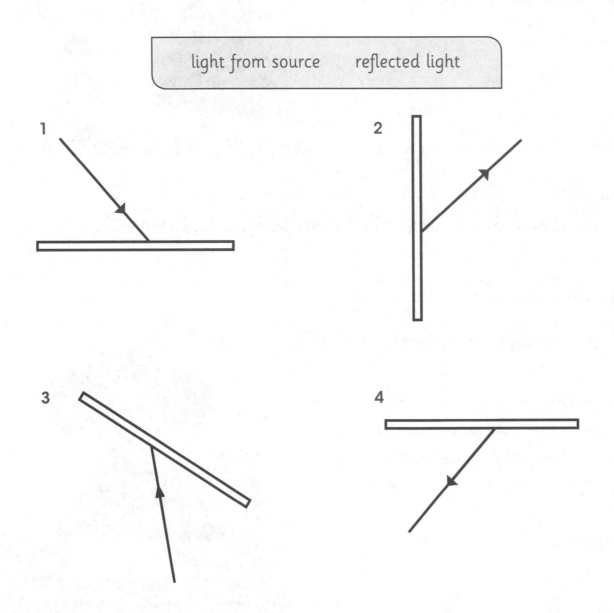

4 The way we see things

Exercise 4.3 Seeing behind you

In this exercise, you will solve a problem using what you have learnt about mirrors.

Ben is sitting underneath the table. His friend, Pablo, puts a can on top of the table, near the edge.

1 What does Ben need in order to see what is on top of the table without moving out from under the table?

_____

2 Draw a labelled diagram to show how Ben can see what is on top of the table.

Exercise 4.4 — Which surfaces reflect light the best?

In this exercise, you will discuss a demonstration to show that some surfaces reflect light better than others.

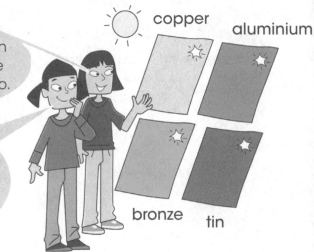

Look at how the sun reflects off all those pieces of metal, Bao.

They are not made of the same metal, Jiao. I bet some of the metals reflect better than others.

copper
aluminium
bronze
tin

1 How can Bao demonstrate to Jiao which metal reflects light the best?

_____

2 Identify two ways in which Bao can make the demonstration a fair test.

_____

_____

_____

3 What conclusion do you think the girls will come to after they have finished their demonstration?

_____

_____

_____

_____

Exercise 4.5   Light changes direction

In this exercise, you will practise what you know about how light changes direction when it reflects off a mirror.

Diagrams 1–6 show light reflecting off mirrors.

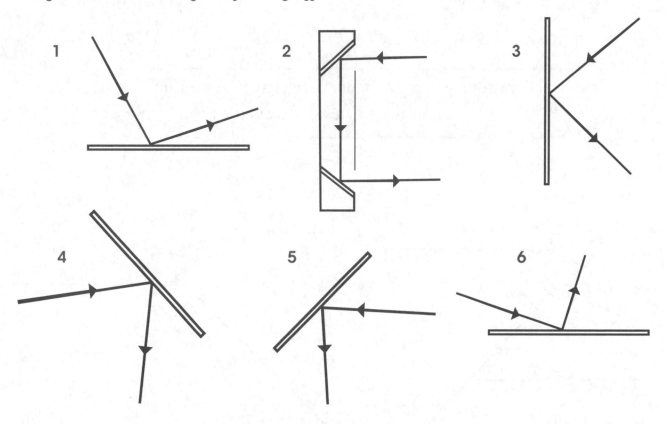

1   Which diagram shows a periscope? _____

2   Which two diagrams are incorrect? _____

3   Re-draw the two diagrams that are incorrect in the space below.
Measure your angles with a protractor.

Language review

This exercise checks that you understand the scientific words used in this unit.

Complete the labels 1–5 on the diagram.

Choose words from this list.

light source   ray   beam   reflects   eyes   mirror
surface   absorb   angle

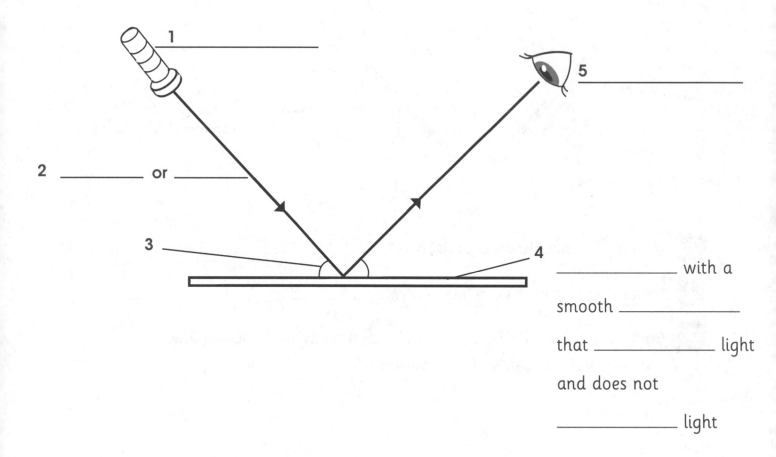

1 _____

2 _____ or _____

3 _____

4 _____ with a

smooth _____

that _____ light

and does not

_____ light

5 _____

Shadows

Exercise 5.1 **Light travels in straight lines**

In this exercise, you will revise what you know about how light travels and how shadows form.

1 Identify the source of light in the picture.

_____

2 The light is blocked by the goat and a shadow forms. The light is also blocked by the hut. Draw the shadow formed by the hut on the picture.

3 Fill in the correct words in this sentence.

Shadows form when light from a light _____ is _____ by a solid object.

4 Fill in the correct words in this sentence.

Light travels in _____ lines.

Exercise 5.2 Which materials let light through?

In this exercise, you will apply what you know about opaque, translucent and transparent materials.

Think of the materials that you need to build a house. You might use bricks, wood, glass and tinted glass. Some parts of the house need to let the light in. But for other parts of the house you need to let no light in, or perhaps just a little light. If you live in a hot place, you may want to make a shady area around your house. If you live in a cold place, you may want to make a sunny area.

Draw a picture of your house in the space below. Label the materials you use.

Complete these sentences.

1 I used _____ to make the _____ so that a lot of light comes in.

2 I used _____ to make the _____ so that some light comes in.

3 I used _____ to make the _____ so that no light comes in.

4 I made a shady area with _____ which blocks _____ light.

or

I made a sunny area with _____ which lets light in.

Exercise 5.3 Silhouettes and shadow puppets

In this exercise, you find out more about silhouettes and answer questions.

If we want a picture of ourselves or our friends, we can take a photograph. Before photography was invented, people had their portraits painted by an artist. This was expensive. Then, in the middle of the 18th century in Europe, people had their portrait cut from black card. This was much cheaper than having a painting done.

These cut out pictures became known as silhouettes. The word 'silhouette' comes from the name of Étienne de Silhouette, a French finance minister. He became very unpopular with the French people because he cut costs, so his name became associated with anything done or made cheaply.

1 Who was Étienne de Silhouette?

_____

2 Why was the portrait cut from black card named after Étienne de Silhouette?

_____

_____

3 Draw a silhouette portrait of a member of your family in the space below.

Exercise 5.4 What affects the size of a shadow?

In this exercise, you will think about what affects the size of a shadow.

Look at the picture of a lamp shining on a mug. A shadow of the mug forms on the screen.

Here is a list of ways in which you could change the size of the shadow. Tick the ways that would make the shadow bigger.

Move the lamp further away from the mug

Move the screen further away from the mug

Move the screen towards the mug

Move the mug further away from the lamp

Move the lamp towards the mug

Move the mug towards the lamp

Exercise 5.5 Investigating shadow lengths

In this exercise, you will think about how the length of a shadow changes at different times of the day.

Janine and Sephora did an investigation to find out how shadow lengths change throughout the day.

They found a bench in the school yard and measured the length of the shadow it made at 08:30.

At lunch time they found people sitting on the bench, but they managed to measure the shadow again. They forgot to note down the time.

At 16:30, they went back to the bench, but it had been moved. They measured the shadow again and noted the time.

1 Do you think they collected enough evidence to make a conclusion about

how shadow lengths change throughout the day? Explain your answer.

_____

_____

2 In what ways was their investigation not a fair test?

_____

_____

_____

3 Predict how the shadow length changed between:

a   08:30 and lunchtime

_____

b   Lunchtime and 16:30.

_____

Exercise 5.6 Measuring light intensity

In this exercise, you will apply what you know about light intensity to analyse some data.

Light intensity can be measured in a unit called a lux.

The table shows some examples of light intensity. The letters A, B, C and D refer to question **2**.

Light intensity in lux	Surfaces lit by
0.002	night sky with no moon
0.27–1.0	A
50	family living room lights
100	B
320–500	office lighting
400	sunrise or sunset on a clear day
1000	C
10 000–25 000	full daylight (not direct sun)
32 000–130 000	D

1 What is light intensity?

_____

2 In the table there are four examples of lit surfaces that have been labelled A,B,C and D.

Predict which of these is:

TV studio lighting _____

Outside on a dark, overcast day _____

Outside when the Moon is full _____

Direct sunlight _____

Exercise 5.7 How scientists measured and understood light

In this exercise, you will read about how scientists invented and improved the light bulb.

Solutions

Sir Joseph Swan was the first to make a light bulb. He used a carbon paper filament. This worked well but burned up very quickly.

In 1878, Thomas Edison improved the electric light bulb. He used a filament wire, but put the filament inside a glass bulb. He replaced the air in the bulb with a special gas that allowed the filament to burn for longer.

Edison experimented with different materials to make a filament produce a brighter light and last longer. First he used a filament made from burnt sewing thread, and then he used bamboo filaments. Soon he had developed a light bulb that lasted 1500 hours.

In 1903, Willis Whitney invented a treatment for the filament so that it wouldn't darken the inside of the bulb as it glowed. In 1910, William David Coolidge invented a tungsten filament.

1 How did Edison and Whitney use creative thinking to improve the light bulb?

_____

_____

_____

_____

Language review

This exercise checks that you understand the scientific words used in this unit.
Answer the clues and complete the word puzzle.

Clues across

1 Our most important light source.

2 A light source you may need to put cells in.

3 Sunglasses are made of this type of glass.

4 A material that will not allow any light pass through it.

5 This has to be transparent so that light can enter the room.

6 The name given to a picture cut from black card to look like a shadow.

7 These materials allow some light to pass through them.

8 Light intensity used to be measured according to this.

9 An opaque object does this to light and causes a shadow to form.

Clue down

1 Used in an experiment to show how the length of a shadow changes throughout the day.

6 Earth's movements

Exercise 6.1 **The Sun, the Earth and the Moon**

In this exercise, you will revise what you know about the movements of the Sun, Earth and Moon.

1 Label the Sun, the Earth and the Moon in the picture.

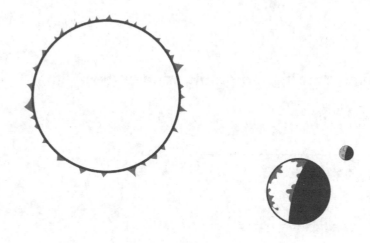

2 Draw and label the orbit made by the Moon and part of the orbit made by the Earth.

Exercise 6.2   Does the Sun move?

In this exercise, you will apply what you know about the apparent position of the Sun in the sky at different times of day.

Look at the pictures of a tree which are labelled 1–5. Each picture shows the Sun in a different position and the shadow of a different length.

Drawing number 1 represents 07:00 in the morning.

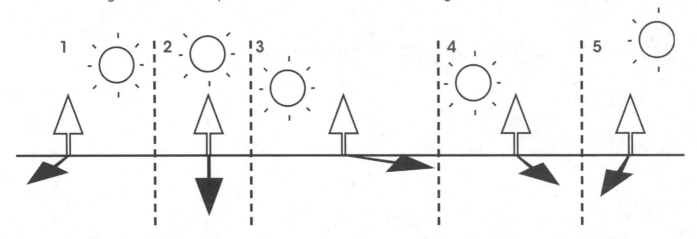

1   **Which drawing represents each of these times?**

   a   **10:00**

   _____

   b   **13:00**

   _____

   c   **16:00**

   _____

   d   **19:00**

   _____

2   **Name the two factors that you used to decide which drawing represented each time.**

   _____

   _____

Exercise 6.3 The Earth rotates on its axis

In this exercise you will compare the rotation of different planets.

Earth is one of the planets in the solar system. All the planets in the solar system rotate on their axis. But they rotate at different speeds. Look at the data in the table. Mercury takes 59 Earth days to make one rotation. This means that one day on Mercury would be like 59 days on Earth!

Planet	Period of rotation in Earth time
Mercury	59 Earth days
Venus	243 Earth days
Earth	24 Earth hours
Mars	24½ Earth hours
Jupiter	10 Earth hours

1 What does rotation mean?

_____

2 When a planet rotates on its axis, what does the half of the planet facing the Sun experience?

_____

3 a Which planet has the longest day?

_____

   b If you lived on this planet, and slept for half the day, how long would you have to sleep for every day?

_____

4 a Which planet has the shortest day?

_____

   b If you lived on this planet, how many hours would you be at school each day if, on Earth, you spend about six hours at school each day?

_____

Exercise 6.4 Sunrise and sunset

In this exercise, you will analyse data about sunrise and sunset.

Here are some data about sunrise and sunset in Karachi, Pakistan.

Date	Sunrise	Sunset	Length of day	Change — is day getting longer or shorter?
March 16th	06:40	18:41	12:01	
+1 day	06:39	18:42		
+1 week	06:33	18:44		
+2 weeks	06:26	18:47		
+1 month	06:10	18:54		
+2 months	05:48	19:09		
+3 months	05:42	19:22		
+6 months	06:18	18:37		

1 How do you work out the length of day?

_____

_____

2 Complete the table by filling in the length of day column. Then write longer or shorter for each line in the last column.

3 Identify the pattern shown by the data between March and June for the length of day.

_____

4 a Is Karachi going from Spring to Summer or from Autumn to Winter between March and June?

_____

b Explain how you know this.

_____

5 Explain the data in the +6 months line.

_____

_____

Exercise 6.5 The Earth revolves around the Sun

In this exercise, you will answer questions about a diagram that shows night and day.

North Pole

Equator

Night

Day

Sun's rays

X

•Y

South Pole

1 **a** Which hemisphere is having summer?

_____

b Explain your answer.

_____

2 **a** Estimate the length of day experienced by people living at X.

_____

b What time will sunrise and sunset be at X?

_____

3 **a** If you lived at Y, would you need a thick coat outside?

_____

b Explain why or why not.

_____

4 Which month of the year does this diagram represent?

_____

Exercise 6.6 Exploring the solar system

In this exercise, you will read about Jupiter and answer questions.

Jupiter is the largest planet in the solar system. Jupiter rotates on its axis once every ten Earth hours. One of Jupiter's revolutions around the Sun takes 12 Earth years.

Jupiter has four large moons, and at least 24 small moons that revolve around it. Jupiter is a gas giant. It consists mainly of two gases, hydrogen and helium, with smaller amounts of other gases in the surface layers.

Robotic probes have been sent to Jupiter. The images sent back by the probes show colourful bands of clouds surrounding Jupiter. No water has been found on Jupiter.

1 a Which star does Jupiter revolve around?

_____

   b How long does one revolution take?

_____

2 Is daytime longer or shorter on Jupiter than it is on Earth?

_____

3 Compare the surfaces of Earth and Jupiter.

_____

4 a How can we continue to find out more about Jupiter and its moons?

_____

   b Do you think it would be possible for a spacecraft to land on Jupiter?

Explain why or why not.

_____

_____

Exercise 6.7　Exploring the stars

In this exercise, you will find out about a telescope in Africa and use your knowledge to answer questions.

Southern African Large Telescope (SALT) is the largest optical telescope in the southern hemisphere and one of the largest in the world. SALT is located in an observatory on high land, 350 km from the nearest city. It was opened in 2005.

The telescope contains 91 mirrors. Each mirror measures 11 m across.

SALT can detect light from distant objects in the universe that are a billion times too faint to be seen with the naked eye.

Astronomers from all over the world come to the observatory to use SALT and do their research. They exchange ideas and work together to explain things they observe.

1 What is an optical telescope?

_____

2 Why is the location of SALT a good place for an optical telescope?

_____

_____

3 What is the purpose of the mirrors in the telescope?

_____

4 Japan, Mongolia and the United Kingdom are all countries in the northern hemisphere. Why do you think astronomers from these countries like to work at the observatory in Southern Africa?

_____

_____

Language review

This exercise checks that you understand the scientific words used in this unit.

1 Here is a picture of the eight planets in the solar system.

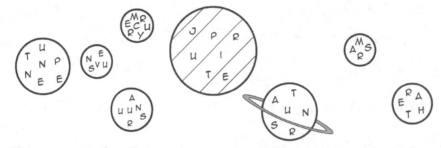

a   Unscramble the names of the planets. Write them in order from the planet closest to the Sun to the planet furthest away from the Sun.

_____

_____

b   Name the **two** movements that each planet makes.

_____

2 Complete these sentences using these words.

> horizon   astronomer   sunrise   appears   galaxies
> sunset   universe   telescopes

You might have to use one more than once.

An _____ studies the stars in _____ in the

_____ .

They use optical _____ to see stars far away.

The Sun _____ to rise above the _____

at _____ and move across the sky to sink below the

_____ at _____ .

CAMBRIDGE PRIMARY
Science

Activity Book 5

Cambridge Primary Science is a flexible, engaging course
written specifically for the Cambridge Primary Science curriculum
framework (Stages 1–6). The course offers plenty of teaching ideas to
give flexibility, allowing teachers to select activities most appropriate to their
classroom and pupils. An enquiry-based style of teaching and learning is stimulated,
with the Scientific Enquiry objectives integrated throughout to encourage learning of
these skills alongside the scientific concepts. The language level is carefully pitched to
be accessible to EAL/ESL learners, with concepts illustrated through diagrams to allow
visual understanding and learning.

The Activity Book contains:

- one exercise to accompany each
  Topic in the Learner's Book
- exercises that can be completed in
  class or as homework
- exercises that are designed to
  consolidate understanding and
  deepen it by applying knowledge in
  new situations
- exercises that practise Scientific
  Enquiry skills
- at the end of each unit, an exercise
  to practise the core vocabulary from
  that unit.

Other components of Cambridge Primary Science 5:

Learner's Book 5   ISBN: 978-1-107-67304-6
Teacher's Resource 5   ISBN: 978-1-107-67673-2

For our full range of Cambridge Primary titles,
including Mathematics, English and
Global English, visit
education.cambridge.org/cambridgeprimary

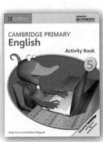
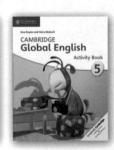

Completely **Cambridge**

Cambridge resources **for** Cambridge qualifications

Cambridge University Press works with Cambridge International Examinations and
experienced authors, to produce high-quality endorsed textbooks and software that
support Cambridge Teachers and encourage Cambridge Learners.

W & G FOYLE

9 781107 658974

18/02/2015
ISBN : 9781107658974 2.50
TITLE: CAMBRIDGE PRIMARY SC
CAT: GKS - KS2 A-Z BY SUBJ